# THE NEW ENEMY

# &

# THE OLD ENEMY

# TOGETHER AT THE GATE

**THE NEW ENEMY**

**&**

**THE OLD ENEMY**

TOGETHER AT THE GATE

ISBN 978-1-990966-90-3

COPYRIGHT 2020 - TREVOR HERBERT
ALL RIGHTS RESERVED

All rights reserved. No part of this publication may be reproduced or transmitted in any form or by any means, electronic or mechanical, including photocopy, recording or any information storage or retrieval system without prior permission from the copyright owner.

Unless otherwise stated, the views expressed in this book are those of the author and he does not claim to speak on behalf of anybody, be that an individual or an organisation.

Dedicated to all those who believe in the power of both words and actions - who have the courage to speak when the hour requires that we break our silence and who then set the example by following through with the requisite action - also as the hour demands it.

*'The pandemic has exposed the plight of the poor and the great inequality that reigns in the world. And the virus, while it does not distinguish between people, has found, in its devastating path, great inequalities and discrimination. And it has exacerbated them!'*

**Pope Francis**

# Praise for The Church, The City & The Virus

*The nature of the book's context and content presupposes a sequel. We are left wondering how the work, witness and ministry of the church will look in a post COVID-19 world.*

**Bruce Theron**
Director: Ekklesia
Faculty of Theology, Stellenbosch University

- - - 0 - - -

*In this book, Trevor Herbert asks some difficult questions regarding the decisions surrounding our nation's response to the COVID-19 epidemic.*

**Graham Power**
Chairman: Power Group
Founder of the Global Day of Prayer and Unashamedly Ethical

- - - 0 - - -

*The book exposes the kind of church we have become. I will advise you to grab yourself a copy!*

**Mbulelo Bikwani**
Executive Director: Sucgrate Consulting Services (Pty) Ltd
Chairman, Western Cape Ecumenical Network (WCEN)

- - - 0 - - -

*The author captures succinctly how secular governments marginalised and disregarded the Church in relegating it to the level of a social event, with regulations more stringent than even that relating to the taxi industry.*

**Alan Platt**
Global Leader Doxa Deo / City Changers

---O---

*The author's agony as a leader is not unique; a similar deafening silence is rife across the [African] continent...*

**Stephen Mbogo**
International CEO
African Enterprise / Lausanne Africa (EPSA) Regional Director

---O---

*Trevor Herbert is an exceptional leader and leader of leaders. If you are passionate about transformation, I wholeheartedly recommend you read his book 'The Church, The City & The Virus'."*

**Matt Bird**
CEO of Cinnamon Network International

# Acknowledgements

This book has been written during a period of extraordinary leave granted to me by our local church for which I will remain eternally grateful. Even before *The Church, The City & The Virus* was published in July 2020, I became seized with the idea of a trilogy which would have to be published within a twelve-month cycle. However, I was convinced that for the sequel to have any meaningful impact, it had to be made available within three months after the first book.

First and foremost, as I have said so many times before, I have to thank God for bestowing on me so much grace that I might be allowed to serve the Church of our Lord Jesus Christ and His people in so many ways and in so many places. Sometimes I think that there is no other person on the planet who is as fulfilled by their calling and vocation as I am, and I occasionally become overwhelmed with a sense of unworthiness about this privilege. Over the last 20 years, as the saying goes, I have not worked a day in my life.

Secondly, as always, a big thank you to those precious souls who have always provided me with an environment of support envied by many - a home and office combined where I am allowed to use my time and pursue those endeavours that I am passionate about - my wife, children and grandchildren. God has blessed me with the grace to travel far and wide across the globe, but there is no greater reward, and nothing gives me greater pleasure, than to return to the inviting warmth and comfort of home.

Finally, I would like to express my sincere gratitude to all of those who have contributed to the successful completion of this work, especially my friend Barend Petersen who has written the foreword to the book. To those behind the scenes who have assisted with the cover photography and design, proofreading, editing and generally making sure that the final product, in addition to hopefully being a good read, also looks good - please receive and accept my most profound gratitude for all your value-adding contributions. God bless you!

*'Global poverty is a complex web of interlinked problems. There is no one "silver bullet" that will solve global inequality. Multiple contributing factors must be tackled in parallel. Yes, education alone is unlikely to lead to employment without economic reform to address the demand side in much of the developing world.'*

***Adam Braun***

# Preface

*'...but when you are old, you will stretch out your hands, and others will dress you and take you where you don't want to go.'*

John 18:21b (NLT)

Stay safe. Stay at home.

This is what the whole world has been told during the greater part of this year, 2020. Lockdown is a term that even both my grandsons of pre-school going age understand. This isolation from the outside world is for our own good, we have been told. And this is probably true. So many millions have been infected by this novel coronavirus, COVID-19. At the time of writing there was more than 35 million infections worldwide[1] and more than a million had already succumbed to this deadly enemy of the human race. The disease has not only been a threat to the health of the global population, but has also left, in its path of destruction, crippled economies and, consequently, has added millions to the already high number of unemployed people in the world.

In my previous work entitled, *The Church, The City & The Virus*[2], I have contended that probably not all countries have always responded to this pandemic in a manner that had the best interests of most of its citizens at heart. In my humble opinion, this is especially true in the case of our own country, South Africa. It appears now, with hindsight, that from the get-go, political opportunists set themselves up to benefit from the plight and suffering of the people of this nation. Heartless and corrupt, politically connected individuals have enriched themselves, their friends and their families at the expense of the poor and the destitute. The extent of the corruption has not only reached to the high heavens, but has also angered a nation already suffering the worst nightmare imaginable.

There are so many sayings and clichés that one can think of that ring chillingly true during these dark days and crazy times. As others have said so many times before, power corrupts, and absolute power corrupts absolutely. Evil triumphs when good people do nothing. Those who are silent when they ought to have spoken and were able to, are taken to agree. In South Africa, now, in this author's view, there remains a confusing silence from very influential and very powerful people whose voices many South Africans have expected to hear. I am not referring to the voices of politicians from opposition parties - sometimes, during this pandemic, politicians opposed to the ruling party have probably made relevant and useful contributions - but one can never be sure whether it is really about the nation's interest or their own narrow interests.

Other good but faint voices have also been heard. There is an organisation named For South Africa or FORSA for short, who have submitted important input to the powers that be, and they should probably be appreciated for that. The South African Council of Churches (SACC) has provided some response as far as the recent wave of corruption is concerned, but the practical possibilities of executing their proposed programme of action has yet to be seen. Many business leaders have spoken - but again, one must hope that it is really about the greater good and in the interest of the vulnerable majority and not about narrow personal, business interest. Trade unions and certain state-salaried employee groups have also made their voices heard. Again, one cannot be sure whether it is out of concern for the nation's interests or self-interest.

South Africa has a history of church leaders who gave clear and sacrificial leadership during the devastating apartheid years. There was not only audible and visible condemnation of the wrongs that were being perpetrated by that evil regime, but the voice of the Church was also accompanied by relentless and unabating efforts to make sure that the resident evil was removed. At great risk to themselves, leaders took to the police and army-filled streets to protest against the abomination that was apartheid. They were locked up, tortured and some even killed by an arrogant system that, for a very long time, refused to listen to the voices of reason. From that evil system, we as a nation, have inherited an unequal society in an unequal world. A world described in detail by the secretary-general of the United Nations during his Nelson Mandela Annual Lecture 2020 speech.[3]

In this work I will often refer to the content of that speech by António Guterres delivered from New York on 18 July 2020. There are several reasons for making significant use of some of the highlights from his speech. In the first place, it was delivered on the commemoration of the birthday of South Africa's most famous icon - our former president, the late Nelson Mandela. In the second place, the title of his paper, 'Tackling the Inequality Pandemic: A New Social Contract for a New Era', speaks directly to the title of this work. In the third place, during his speech he alluded to most of the salient aspects regarding the prevailing inequality in our world and how the new enemy, COVID-19 has 'shone a spotlight on this injustice': He refers to a range of topical issues including, but not limited to the collapse of health and economic systems, gender inequality, wealth and poverty, food and social security as well as the imbalance in 'global power relations'.

Not in our wildest nightmares could we have imagined that when the evil called COVID-19 sprung its surprise attack on us, all across the globe, it would be joined by our old enemy of inequality - now mutated into its most lethal strain where even some of our own have demonstrated that they believe that they are more equal than the rest of us and that they and their friends have a right to squander the resources of a whole nation, as is the example in our country, South Africa. But perhaps, in all of this, there is an opportunity that presents itself to the Church of our Lord Jesus Christ to not only be the voice of the voiceless, but also the voice of reason and sanity.

31 October 2020

Cape Town, South Africa

# Foreword

Besides his relationships with his family and friends that he cherishes so deeply, there are three other things that Trevor Herbert is passionate about and that is the Church of our Lord Jesus Christ, his city and the global community. And the role he believes the Church is called to fulfil in transforming our communities, our cities and our world until hopefully, it may be 'on earth as it is heaven'. This is revealed every time when Herbert puts pen to paper. In his first publication during 1994 and in his recent work, *The Church, The City & The Virus*, the theme of organisational and community transformation comes through.

Now, in his latest work, *The New Enemy & The Old Enemy - Together at the Gate*, Herbert is again drawing his readers' attention to the further delays to the global transformation project caused by the lethal collaboration between the novel coronavirus called COVID-19 and the worldwide phenomenon of economic inequality, as well as other forms of inequality. But he goes further than that. Herbert also offers his views on how the Church can and should become a more audible voice and demonstrate a more visible presence as far as the global response to these 'two enemies at the gate' are concerned.

Herbert has a passion for people, especially those who find themselves on the fringes of society - the powerless and the voiceless, the poor and the marginalised, the forlorn and the forgotten. He has passed by several opportunities to minister in the more affluent local churches of his denomination because, like Moses, he prefers to 'suffer with the people'. His writing always comes from this place. In his own words from chapter 18, like the prophet Jeremiah, he is driven by a 'fire in his bones' and like Jeremiah, speaking from this 'fire', he has perhaps opened himself up to the risk of being 'misunderstood'.

But Herbert has also made sure that his readers are made aware that he is not alone in his concern for the inequalities that prevail in our world - and how these inequalities have been exacerbated by the devastation caused by the novel coronavirus and COVID-19. In this regard he has provided his readership with a list of sources and resources where we are able to see for ourselves that others before him have highlighted the very same issues that he is drawing our attention to. And in addition to this, he has strategically placed some quotations by well-known and lesser known individuals all over this work – in particular the opening quote by Pope Francis.

Finally, the author comes back to the point that the Church has a role to play in all of this and that an opportunity in this regard is presenting itself at the present time. The author is insisting that like Queen Esther in the Old Testament and the city of Jerusalem in the New Testament, the globe in general and the Church, in particular, are facing some kind of Kairos moment that should not be taken lightly. Herbert is not asking us to agree with him. He is asking us where we stand and how we will respond. And as strategically placed as his opening quote is, is the final three worded challenge directly to each reader from his closing quote by Megan Markle – 'why not me'?

**Barend Petersen**
B Compt. (Hons) CA (SA)
Chairman, Macrovest Capital

*'How can we effect change in the world when only half of it is invited or feel welcome to participate in the conversation? ...'*

**Emma Watson**

# Table of Contents

**Introduction**..................................................................1

**Chapter 1**....................................................................6
   An Unequal World

**Chapter 2**..................................................................10
   The Speech of the UN Sectary-General

**Chapter 3**..................................................................14
   The Rich and the Poor

**Chapter 4**..................................................................18
   Unequal Power Relations

**Chapter 5**..................................................................22
   Abuse of Power / Corruption

**Chapter 6**..................................................................26
   So Much Information – The Devil is in the Detail

**Chapter 7**..................................................................30
   The Effect on the Church

**Chapter 8**..................................................................34
   The Church and Her Internal Struggles

**Chapter 9**..................................................................38
   The End of Poverty?

**Chapter 10**................................................................42
   COVID-19 – The New Enemy

**Chapter 11**................................................................46
   COVID-19 Conspiracies

**Chapter 12**...........................................................50
    Inequality – The Old Enemy

**Chapter 13**...........................................................54
    Paralysis by Analysis

**Chapter 14**...........................................................58
    The Scoreboard

**Chapter 15**...........................................................62
    A few Good People

**Chapter 16**...........................................................66
    The Time is Right

**Chapter 17**...........................................................70
    Re-imagining the Future

**Chapter 18**...........................................................75
    A Better World

**Chapter 19**...........................................................79
    An Opportunity for the Church

**Chapter 20**...........................................................83
    Doing the Right Thing

**Chapter 21**...........................................................87
    How Will the Church Respond?

**Afterword**............................................................91

**References**...........................................................94

# Introduction

*'A double standard of weights and measures
- both are disgusting to the Lord.'*

Proverbs 20:10 God's Word Translation (GWT)

The evil twins. COVID-19 and inequality.

The one arrived long before the other. But when the other showed up on the scene, the first was exposed in all its nakedness. All over the planet, wherever the second twin planted its devastating footprints, the other was revealed in all the same kinds of places where similar living conditions prevailed. Wherever there was poverty the twins left a trail of suffering and devastation. It seemed that the threat to food and job security would overwhelm the dangers that presented themselves as far as the health of the world's poorest communities was concerned. The crippling of economies all over the world seemed to present the very real danger of extended years of worsening global poverty and inequality.

Year after year, ironically, in one of the richest countries in the world, Switzerland, global leaders meet and reflect on the so-called common challenges that face humanity. Unavoidably, at the top of that list of challenges should be inequality, poverty and unemployment. Imagine, the business and political elite gathering in one of the wealthiest corners on the globe to talk about extreme poverty and the growing gap between the haves and the have nots. As someone once remarked, 'over expensive steaks in luxury hotels, they discuss the problem of world hunger'. It appears, if the lack of significant progress in the world is anything to go by, that every time they seem to emerge with the poorest solutions!

The World Economic Forum (WEF)[4], a non-governmental organisation (NGO), was founded in January 1971 by Klaus Schwab and has its headquarters in Cologny, Switzerland. The mission of the organisation is to 'improve the state of the world by engaging business, political, academic, and other leaders of society to shape global, regional, and industry agendas'. The mission of the WEF is succinctly summarised in the motto of the NGO, 'committed to improving the state of the world'. Over time, the WEF has endured its fair share of criticism and controversy, famously being described as 'a place where billionaires tell millionaires what the middleclass feels'.

Every year the WEF hosts a meeting in Davos, Switzerland, where ways and means are discussed on how the state of the world can be improved. During its meeting in January 2020, amongst other, the following threats to the future of the global family was identified. It is instructive to observe that the evil triplets of poverty, inequality and unemployment is not listed amongst the top five global risks discussed during that meeting. In fact, the top five risks are all so-called environmental risks such as extreme weather events, the failure of climate change mitigation, human-made environmental damage and disasters, major biodiversity loss and ecosystem collapse, as well as major natural disasters.

From Davos, Switzerland to New York, United States of America (USA) - in another city, another organisation that is trying to make a difference in the world has its headquarters. The United Nations[5] was founded on 24 October 1945 in San Francisco, California in the USA. It is a so-called intergovernmental organisation that aims to 'maintain international peace and security, develop friendly relations amongst nations, achieve international cooperation, and be a centre for harmonising the actions of nations'. The current secretary-general is António Guterres and he, on the contrary (as opposed to the latest list of risks from the WEF) has highlighted the aspect of global inequality in July 2020.

During his address at the virtual Nelson Mandela Annual Lecture held on 18 July 2020 (the commemoration of the late icon's birthday) António Guterres entitled his speech, 'Tackling the Inequality Pandemic: A New Social Contract for a New Era'. In his speech he reminds the global family of the conditions that prevailed before the devastating arrival of the novel coronavirus and COVID-19, and how the pandemic has contributed to the dramatic worsening of the already fragile state of the global economy of an unsuspecting global population and the subsequent devastating effects on the poorest communities of the world.

It seems that the collaboration between the new enemy called COVID-19 and the old enemy of inequality will be with us for some time still and that they will leave more casualties than what we could ever imagine. How will we (the global family) respond to these two enemies at the gate? The one observation (amongst other) shared by Carmen Cervone & Andrea Scatolon (edited by Mitch Brown)[6] in an article entitled, 'The Inequality Paradox, Inequality Awareness, and System Justification', is that there is no collective struggle against the old enemy of inequality. Brown and his colleagues speculate that this behaviour might be because of a lack of awareness and knowledge about the old enemy.

On the other hand, the focus of the collective global effort against the new enemy called COVID-19 seems to suggest that this is currently the only one clear and present danger at the gate - only one visible enemy. Every day for the last number of months, the world has been kept informed and aware of the finest detail about the advance of COVID-19 against humanity - so many new infections, so many recoveries, so many deaths - a high level of global awareness of the enemy's presence and tactics. Perhaps this type of response might help to clarify why there is no similar collective global effort as far as the threat from growing inequality is concerned. That may be due to a much lower level of global awareness about the presence and tactics of this other older, almost invisible enemy joined by COVID-19, now together at the gate.

*'A nation will not survive morally or economically when so few have so much and so many have so little.'*

**Bernie Sanders**

# 1

## An Unequal World

*'The rich rule over the poor, and the borrower is slave to the lender.'*

Proverbs 22:7 (NIV)

What did the world look like when the new enemy, COVID-19, arrived on the scene?

The world as we know it is a place of stark and glaring inequality. All over the globe there are examples of extreme wealth and extreme poverty. In some of the world's nations it would almost be impossible to come by on 3 000 dollars for the month, while in many other parts of the planet people are barely scraping by on less than a dollar a day - a stark reminder of the words of our Lord Jesus Christ Himself, 'the poor you have with you always'.[7] And while we are quoting from the good Book, let us also be reminded of the words of the wise old Solomon, 'when the poor beg for mercy the rich answer sharply'.[8]

Almost half of the world's wealth is in the hands of less than ten people. On the other hand, in shrill contrast, it seems that half of the world's poorest people live in less than ten countries. It is estimated that of the world's 736 million extreme poor in 2015, 368 million - half of the total - lived in just five countries.[9] Those countries with the highest number of extreme poor are India, Nigeria, Democratic Republic of

Congo, Ethiopia and Bangladesh. Coincidentally, these countries are also the most populous countries of South Asia and Sub-Saharan Africa - the two regions that together account for 85% (629 million) of the world's poor. Besides these, there are so many other different examples of inequality all over the world.

Often inequality is manifested along race, class and gender lines. Exceptions aside, this has been a global phenomenon as old as humanity itself. I often wonder what exactly our Lord Jesus Christ meant when he said, 'the poor you have with you always'. In the same manner as wealth is handed down from generation to generation, so poverty is also handed down. It seems that the child of a worker is condemned to be a worker. The child of a very poor person will end up a very poor person. The opportunities to which the children of the wealthy will be exposed, will empower them to have a much more positive and entrepreneurial outlook on life, whereas the child of the poor person will probably have honed only the basic survival skills.

To highlight an example of brutal unfairness and inequality, in South Africa there is the situation of the descendants of the first people who lived in the country and their long and hard fight for fair treatment. There are many who regard the descendants of the San and Khoi people as the rightful first inhabitants[10] of the land and, therefore, its rightful owners. But to see the living conditions of the confirmed heirs of those first inhabitants is another example of how the rich and powerful can get away with taking that which is not rightfully theirs and then still boast about the pittance that their forbears paid for their property.

The footprints of the old enemy of inequality may, historically, even be traced to the Church of our Lord Jesus Christ. In my earlier work[11] I alluded to the fact that within large denominations the effects of both the lockdown regulations and the health risks of the COVID-19 virus were vastly different in the more affluent suburbs than in the poorer neighbourhoods. By and large, it was blue collar workers who were the hardest hit by the devastation caused by short time, retrenchment and unemployment. The socio-economic knock-on effects on the church was equally devastating. It made very little sense to pastors who were grappling without income and food on their tables how their colleagues in the suburbs were able to continue their vocation with little or no negative effects on their livelihoods.

In some quarters it is argued that the novel coronavirus and the disease that it carries, COVID-19, is just a relative of the common flu and if a young, healthy person would be infected with the virus, after some days of isolation, the virus would leave and look for another victim. Within this school of thought COVID-19 is labelled an opportunistic disease and these experts maintain that, when the dreaded virus stumbles on an older person with one or more underlying conditions, it is at its deadliest. The often-fatal harm that COVID-19 inflicts on its victim is always in collaboration with an underlying condition of some or other kind.

Ironically, the same kind of logic seems to apply to certain historically disadvantaged communities, neighbourhoods and groups. When the lethal disease visits their part of the world it often finds underlying socio-economic conditions with which it can collaborate to cause far more devastation than it would be able to in a more affluent and better prepared environment. All over the world, wherever the pre-existing conditions were in their favour, the two evil twins of COVID-19 and inequality, in the most calculating manner, seemed to have left their malicious footprints and have set back the socio-economic recovery of those poor communities by decades, at the very least.

*'In a world where vows are worthless. Where making a pledge means nothing. Where promises are made to be broken, it would be nice to see words come back into power.'*

**Chuck Palahniuk**

# 2

## The Speech of the UN Secretary-General

*'Our courts oppose the righteous, and justice is nowhere to be found. Truth stumbles in the streets, and honesty has been outlawed.'*

Isaiah 59:14 (NLT)

During his speech at the Nelson Mandela Annual Lecture on 18 July 2020, the secretary-general of the United Nations reminded all of us of the many ways in which inequality has impacted the world as we know it and that it has reached crisis proportions around the world in the recent decades and that this crisis poses a growing threat to our future. He goes on to suggest ways on how we can address the many mutually reinforcing strands and layers of inequality, before they destroy our economies and societies, having aptly entitled his speech, 'Tackling the Inequality Pandemic - A New Social Contract for a New Era'.

In his introduction he heaped well deserved praise on the late former president of South Africa, Nelson Mandela for rising above his jailers to liberate millions of South Africans and then went on to become both a global inspiration and a modern icon. Guterres acknowledged Madiba (his clan name, by which the late president is affectionately known) for having devoted his life to fighting the inequality that has reached crisis proportions around the world in recent decades – and that poses a growing threat to our future. As stated in the opening paragraph of this chapter, the good secretary-general then proceeded to talk about ways in which the global community can address, as he put it, 'the mutually reinforcing strands and layers of inequality' that exist in our world.

Like a good bureaucrat, the United Nations secretary-general touched on most, if not all, of the aspects of the lives of global citizens that have been affected by what he calls the inequality pandemic. He referred to economies in free fall and how the world has been brought to its knees by a microscopic virus causing a pandemic which has demonstrated the fragility of our world. Using the inclusive pronoun, we, without seemingly apportioning any blame to anyone, he listed examples of the risks we have ignored for decades. Amongst other, he referred to many of the aspects that were exposed right here in our home country, South Africa, like inadequate health systems, gaps in social protection, structural inequalities, environmental degradation, climate crisis etc.

A part of his speech that those of us living in the poorer parts of the world should note with great concern, is that the poor and vulnerable communities of the world should expect delays as far as the global goals, which powerful individuals and organisations have envisaged for the poorer parts of our world, is concerned. In his speech António Guterres issues a veiled warning to the poor when he cautions that regions that were making progress on eradicating poverty and narrowing inequality have been set back years in a matter of months and that the world is facing the deepest global recession since World War II, and the broadest collapse in incomes since 1870.

Words are not without power - as the saying goes, there is power in the spoken word. And the good secretary-general has clearly said all the right things and touched on most, if not all, matters that deserve our urgent attention. Now, hopefully, these words will be acted upon by those with the influence, power and authority to make all the desired outcomes a reality. Organisations like the United Nations, the WEF and other powerful individuals and institutions who have, up to now, received their fair share of criticism for their long-standing inability or unwillingness to seriously move forward, will now hopefully move from words and clichés to more meaningful and sustainable action.

*'An imbalance between rich and poor is the oldest and most fatal ailment of all republics.'*

**Plutarch**

# 3

# The Rich and the Poor

*'The poor plead for mercy; the rich answer with insults.'*

Proverbs 18:23 (NLT)

In our world there are rich nations and there are poor nations. There are rich people and there are poor people.

It seems that this is just the way it is, to echo an expression recently used by a well-known US politician. On the World Wide Web there are many online sources and resources where one may find information about the richest and poorest countries and individuals in the world. Different organisations apply different methodologies and formulae when they make their calculations. As a result, these lists may differ significantly. On 3 August 2020[12] an online magazine calling themselves *Global Finance* who provides global news and insight for corporate financial professionals, published a list of the 'top 10 richest countries in the world'.

What is interesting about the above-mentioned list is that the USA and China are nowhere to be found while on other lists these two countries are placed in first and second wealthiest positions. This other list[13] of the richest nations is led by the USA, China and Japan. Following them are Germany, the United Kingdom (UK), France, India, Italy, Canada and Spain. This second (other) list is published by an organisation called

Credit Suisse as part of their annual 'global wealth report'. According to this report, the USA, as a nation, owns about 30% of the total wealth of the planet. It is also noteworthy to learn that the 500 wealthiest people in the world, together, own almost more than 50% of the total wealth of the entire African continent.

Having mentioned Africa, let us now turn our attention to the poorest countries on the planet. In an article published in *USA Today*[14] the ten poorest countries in the world include countries like Liberia, the Central African Republic, Burundi, the Democratic Republic of the Congo, Niger, Malawi, Mozambique, Sierra Leone, Madagascar and the Comoros Islands. Again, there would be other lists that may be different from this list, based on the calculations and formulae used. The reason that I have listed all 10 of them here is to drive home the point that all of them are on the continent of Africa. It is this wide gap between the richest and the poorest whether continents, nations or individuals that, in my humble opinion, present the leaders of our time with one of their most daunting global challenges - in spite of the fact that it was undermentioned at the WEF meeting in January 2020.

Research will show that not everyone shares this author's view that the ever-widening gap between the rich and the poor should be a high global priority. An article published by *much.net* poses the question, 'why is there no collective struggle towards greater equality, just as there is for other issues such as climate change or equal rights?' The agenda of the WEF meeting held in Davos during January 2020, bears out the fact that issues like climate change are considered a far higher priority for the rich and powerful than the age-old phenomenon of inequality. What I am trying to get my head around is that the effort of eradicating inequality, may be exclusive to the pursuit of equal rights. Surely, equal rights should include the idea of greater economic equity or at least inequality?

The same article highlights other important issues regarding inequality. For example, the levels of awareness and the extent of which the reality of economic equality is widely underestimated. The compilers of the article seem to suggest that knowledge should be the solution to the problem of unawareness. The authors address matters like attitudes towards inequality across nations and cultural contexts. In addition to this, I am sure that many readers are aware of favourite or pet doctrines that propagate a theology which holds that being rich or poor is a spiritual condition manifested in the natural. That people are poor because of a poverty mindset, and that those who are wealthy have the mind of the wealthy.

According to this school of thought, the Biblical warning is a self-fulfilling prophecy - the rich rule over the poor. So, it is all making perfect sense - it is really no use bothering too much about inequality.

*'Money creates a power relationship between the payer and the payee.'*

**Joichi Ito**

# 4

# Unequal Power Relations

*'Don't I have the right to do what I want with my own money? Or are you envious because I am generous?'*

Matthew 20:15 (NIV)

What does Bill Gates do with his money?

In the twentieth chapter of Matthews's gospel, our Lord Jesus Christ tells the parable of the workers who were hired at different times of the same day. Some started at six in the morning, some at nine others at twelve noon. There were even those who started only an hour before the workday ended at about six in the evening. The person handing out the day's wages was instructed to pay a full day's wage to all the workers irrespective of the time that they had started. Those workers who started at six in the morning were extremely unhappy and lodged a complaint with the owner of the vineyard. The owner's response was that he could do with his money whatever he wanted to.

So, what does Bill Gates and others who are equally rich and powerful do with their money? The answer seems to have been hiding in the gospel of Matthew for almost two thousand years - the rich and powerful do with their money pretty much whatever they want to. Even when they are being generous and doing good. Like the vineyard owner in the story, they will decide where and how they will spend their wealth. High on the list of the many good things that Bill Gates and his wife have become involved with, is world health. In this regard, they have done much which has earned high praise and criticism in almost equal measure. So, when the novel coronavirus arrived on the world stage it was inevitable that Bill and Belinda Gates would appear in the frame.

Since a statement made in early 2017[15], Bill Gates has enjoyed a lot of attention from his detractors who have gone to great lengths to make the world aware that Bill Gates had already warned the world years ago about the threat of a planned pandemic. There are videos circulating on social media that, in addition to the above speech, also speculates about the fact that Gates (through his father) has historical links to China, and that both he and his wife are supporters of reducing the world population through medical interventions. Regarding the latter, the Gates couple are accused of being responsible for hundreds, if not thousands, of poor women having lost their babies due to these medical interventions.

These detractors also go to great lengths to bring another name into the equation, namely that of Dr Anthony Fauci, who coincidentally and almost ironically, during the same month in 2017[16] when Gates warned of the threat of a planned pandemic, warned of a surprise outbreak during the Trump administration. It is further speculated that the three are closely linked and that Gates and Fauci, together with other powerful and connected individuals, are busy with a master plan to track and control all the inhabitants of planet earth, and that the alleged planned outbreak of the novel coronavirus is a dress rehearsal for a later complete takeover of human freedoms.

Ironically, it is an annual report published by the Bill & Melinda Gates Foundation called the 'Goalkeepers Report'[17] that shines a revealing light on the gaps that exist between the most powerful and the most vulnerable communities of the world. It is within the pages of this document that we are reminded that a worldwide economic stimulus initiative of at least 18 trillion US dollars was launched to keep countries afloat during and after the pandemic. It is the same report that also reminds us that there are about 68 million people in the world who live below the poverty line on an income of about three US dollars a day and another 37 million people who live below the extreme poverty line on less than two US dollars a day.

The compilers of the 'Goalkeepers Report' describe the expression 'falling below the poverty line' as scratching and clawing every single moment just keep one's family alive. It may benefit the interested reader to study the mentioned report in more detail. This author would risk speculating that the figure of just over 100 million people living below the poverty line, provided in the report, is probably significantly understated and that the real picture might look far worse. And lest we forget, the numbers above refer to only those who live below the so-called poverty line. It is probably safe to assume that there are billions of poor people in the world - not millions.[18]

*'It is hard to imagine a more stupid or more dangerous way of making decisions than by putting those decisions in the hands of people who pay no price for being wrong.'*

**Thomas Sowell**

# 5

## Abuse of Power / Corruption

> *'But he told them, "The kings of the unbelievers lord it over them, and those who exercise authority over them are called benefactors."'*
>
> Luke 22:25 (ISV)

Power corrupts and absolute power corrupts absolutely.

After half a year of lockdown regulations in South Africa and the transfer of parliamentary power to a group of people calling themselves the Command Council on COVID-19[19], there are many who are wondering how many decisions taken by this group has really been in the best interest of the South African nation. It is probably correct to say that, right in the beginning, during the first weeks of the lockdown period in South Africa, the president of the country was able to engage the whole national as a partner in social contract to ward off the worst that the novel coronavirus could potentially inflict upon us as a nation. The people seemed to believe wholeheartedly that their president and his team were acting in their best interest.

At the time of writing, our country found itself in the middle of an unprecedented nationwide reaction against the continuing shameless acts of corruption by politically connected individuals. The chairperson of an ongoing commission of enquiry into the capture of the South African state, Judge Raymond Zondo declared his amazement and disbelief that people are continuing with their brazen acts of greed and corruption. While the economy continued its free-fall and the people continued to suffer under the subsequent avalanche of job losses, the looting apparently also continued unabated. It seemed as if those connected to the ruling elite through either family relations or friendship were smiling all the way to the bank.

It should be remembered that those in political power were ideally and strategically positioned to benefit from a state of disaster, if they would be so inclined. Due to their political proximity, some individuals would have had privileged and early access to important information. Amongst other, that the rules and process which usually applied to state tenders would be waived during the state of disaster and the business could almost exclusively be handed to friends and family. When a certain politician was confronted about this kind of nepotism, the arrogant response was indignant surprise that anything could be wrong with what was going on.

Before Level 5 of lockdown was introduced at midnight on 26 March 2020, almost ten[20] million South Africans were already unemployed. Since then, it has been estimated that another three million[21] have been added to this number. There are those who hold the view that even these figures may be understated. The impact on households have been devastating, to say the least. It has been reported in the news that a single commercial bank has repossessed hundreds of cars and homes since the nation has been under lockdown. The new enemy has shone a harsh light on the huge gap between the powerful and the powerless.

Regulations that seem to make no sense continued to remain in force. One would be allowed to commute in a minibus taxi filled to 100% capacity, but only 50 people would be able to gather in a church building of any size. Even in a three thousand-seater auditorium only 50 (later 250) people would be allowed during a service with very stringent conditions, when for example compared to a shopping mall or supermarket. On the other hand, casinos are permitted to allow entrance to patrons based on the available floor space. For a long time, it remained unlawful to sell tobacco products and cigarettes, but all around the country lawbreaking smokers were merrily puffing away on cigarettes that they had obtained by illegal means.

Since March 2020, in South Africa, all the authority to enforce all the above-mentioned conflicting and confusing legislation rested in the hands of only a few powerful individuals. This author is reminded of an article on the front page of the *Business Day* newspaper published on Friday, 4 September 2020.[22] There was a tiny news column under the heading 'COVID graft a major blemish on Africa'. After an acknowledgement that the continent has dealt with the threat of the novel coronavirus far more effectively than most experts had feared, the article goes on to highlight the one minor detail where Africa comes short - the management of corruption. The front-page summary continues on the inner pages of the paper, focusing on corruption in Kenya, Botswana, Zimbabwe and last, but certainly not least, South Africa.

*'Of all the forms of inequality, injustice in healthcare is the most shocking and inhumane.'*

**Martin Luther King (Jr.)**

# 6

# So Much Information - The Devil is in the Detail

*'Set your mind on things above, not on things on the earth.'*

Colossians 3:2 (NKJV)

Focus, they say.

But on what?

There is a saying, 'you can thank me later'. And one day, perhaps we will thank those who fed us with information through all the social networks during the greater part of the year 2020. Not everything we were told turned out to be factually correct, but not everything turned out to be incorrect either. Take for example those who tried so hard to focus our attention on all the other things that killed people on our planet every year - everything from disease to crime to snakebites. There were even those who checked up on the veracity of these sources and, surprisingly, it turned out that there seems to have been more instances of confirmation of the information than findings of incorrect or inaccurate information, especially the information provided about deaths through diseases other than COVID-19.

Every year, so many people die of so many diseases. The numbers may even be described as staggering. How many of us are aware that about 50 000 people die every day of cardiovascular diseases (about 18 million per year) and more than 25 000 die every day of cancer (about 9 million a year)?[23] At the time of writing, COVID-19 deaths were standing at about one million to date. Counting from 1 January 2020, that is an average of only 4 000 per day. It could be argued that there is a big difference between the type of viral infection spread by the novel coronavirus and the diseases that I have mentioned, but that is not the aspect to which I hope to draw my readers' attention. The point I am trying to make is that our attention was, and is not, drawn to the other diseases daily.

On the contrary, over the last seven months or more, every day, every week and every month the world has been painfully reminded of exactly how many had been infected, how many died and how many recovered from the effects of the deadly disease now infamously known as COVID-19. Why was this daily dose of information important, bearing in mind that the human mind is easily manipulated by information and that fear has been proven to be a great motivator if the intention is to achieve a specific change in human behaviour? I am curious about what the views of the so-called experts would be on this matter. What has the effect been of this daily dose of information about COVID-19 on the human psyche?

There is no getting away from the fact. The human mind is a powerful thing, and it is an equally powerful tool in the hands of unscrupulous manipulators. If the mind can be conditioned to believe that there is a threat in the external environment, then fear becomes the next powerful tool in the arsenal of ruthless individuals who care for no one's interest but their own. But, let there be no doubt - the threat of the disease called COVID-19 is very real. The death of about one million people, with millions more who have been infected, should be a wakeup call to those radical conspiracy theorists who maintain that all of this has been a hoax. However, is it unreasonable to wonder aloud about what is really going on around here?

Over the last decade or two there have been other deadly pandemics that have come and gone. Perhaps this author was not paying close attention back then, but I seem to have no recollection of the daily dose of information about infection, death and dying - a daily cocktail of statistics that increases fear instead of making it subside. Let us also not forget the concomitant effects on the health and livelihoods of the most vulnerable people all over the world. Finally, what is the impact this daily dosage of fear has had on the Church and her adherents? Many of those who may be described as the most committed disciples of our Lord Jesus Christ have been in hiding since they have been fed this daily dose of fear and uncertainty. It seems that the work of the fear mongers has been so complete that, even now when they can come out, these dear children of our Lord still prefer to remain in hiding.

*'There's no doubt that inequality destabilises societies.
I think the social science evidence on that front is crystal clear.'*

**Jordan Peterson**

# 7

## The Effect on the Church

*'For if these things are done when the tree is green, what will happen when it is dry?'*

Luke 23:31 (NLT)

In my earlier work I alluded to the fact that the Church is at its most effective when she has access to people. In the first place, she needs access to the disciples of the movement started by our Lord Jesus Christ.[24] The Biblical mandate is to equip these kingdom workers and keep them sharp for the task laid upon the Church by the Master of the movement. Yes, a movement. An organisation on the go. The workers are equipped internally to be deployed externally. The gathering inside is no less important than the work outside. Having been reduced to a social gathering all over the world and excluding online activity, the Church has not been able to sustain her real work of training and mobilisation.

Perhaps the agents of God's kingdom here on earth should pay attention to some of the so-called best practices going on around us here in the earthly kingdom. Allow me to again draw the readers' attention to the annual 'Goalkeepers Report' of the Bill & Belinda Gates Foundation. In their most recent report (2020), they disclose the purpose of the report and I quote verbatim, 'The point of the report is to track (and promote) progress toward the Sustainable Development Goals, and the big thing standing in the way of that progress right now is the pandemic'. The report provides an important insight into the current world situation, 'we have been set back about 25 years in about 25 weeks'.

In my view, the report contains very useful information. But to which report do we turn to find out what the effect has been on the work of the Church over the last 25 weeks? And what is the extent of the setback to, for example, the primary assignment of the Church which is the advancement of the Biblical mandate to 'go into all the world and make disciples of all nations and teach them to obey everything that the Master of the movement has taught us'? Perhaps another 25 years? And if the current situation is only half as gloomy as the picture painted in the 'Goalkeepers Report', does it make sense if, after all of this, the Church of our Lord Jesus Christ (without relevant information at her disposal) is making big plans to return to church as usual?

Besides the delays that may have been caused by lockdown to the carrying out of the Great Commission, let us not forget that for a long time now, without much success or progress, the Church has been dealing with internal struggles of her own as far as inequality is concerned. The global leader of an organisation called City Changers[25] recently remarked that if the Church does not deal with its own challenges first, it will become very difficult for the Church to make any meaningful impact outside of the church walls. Make no mistake, the Church has always done, continues to do and will probably always be making a huge contribution towards making the world a better place.

This I have witnessed firsthand through my involvement with leaders and movements all over the world. But how sustainable is it for the Church of our Lord Jesus Christ when, for example, in the same denomination, the cost of education is the same for all pastors, but after qualifying, the one leader earns a salary of more than 5 000 dollars and the other a salary of less than 250 dollars per month? And where the one lives in a comfortable double story home in the suburbs and the other in a wooden shack in an informal settlement? Where the one family always has enough to eat, and the other family goes without a meal on many days of the month? How will the Church make a real impact on the detrimental effects of inequality outside if inequality continues behind the stained-glass windows?

*'As long as poverty, injustice and gross inequality persist in our world, none of us can truly rest.'*

**Nelson Mandela**

# 8

# The Church and Her Internal Struggles

> *'It is written,"he said to them, My house will be called a house of prayer, but you are making it a den of robbers."'*
>
> Matthew 21:13 (NIV)

For a long time now, the Church has agonised over her role and influence in matters that affect the lives of all people all over the world and not only the adherents of the Church. The Church, based on the instruction of her founder and leader at the end of Matthew's gospel[26], could be described as a global exporter. Within the body of believers, we often hear talk of taking the whole Gospel to the whole world. But, regrettably so, as mentioned before, for an equally long time, the Church has also been fighting her own internal demons, in a manner of speaking. And perhaps it is the failure of the Church to deal decisively with the enemy within, that has hampered the exporting efforts of the Church.

This author has always maintained that the Church has a duty to respond to acts of mismanagement and corruption by governments and others in positions of authority. Even those within her own ranks. In our country, South Africa, during the first few months of the pandemic and the subsequent lockdown rules and regulations, there was very little, if any, response from the Church to the conflicting, confusing and discriminatory regulations that were being enacted and changed at will. Only much later, after the public outcry against the blatant and arrogant acts of corruption perpetrated by those who enjoyed the privilege and benefits of political proximity, was there some response from the Church and her leaders.

It remains a pity that there still appears to be no clear and unequivocal denouncing and condemnation of the unequal treatment of unequals during the pandemic. Instead, the Church, it seems, is trying to mobilise the citizens to do things for themselves. In other words, those without power are supposed to demonstrate power through peaceful protest and rearranging chairs around on the deck of the sinking Titanic, as responsibly as they can. This public participation will ostensibly have a better lasting effect than a clearly articulated position by the Church on corruption and continuous follow-through to make sure that justice is served for those who believe that they are more equal than others.

It is my firm personal conviction that the voice of the Church should be heard in national and international affairs, especially when the hour demands it. Such an hour was thrust upon the whole of humanity during the year 2020. In some nations of the world the situation was screaming to the highest heavens for a prophetic intervention from the Church of our Lord Jesus Christ. There have been so many leadership moments where the gap in the wall was frighteningly visible. This is also true for our own country, South Africa. We will have to wait and see how the generations who come after us will evaluate the response of the Church during this dark hour. Hopefully we might not have to face the charge that the silence lasted too long before the Church spoke up a little louder.

But for what it is worth, in the end, the Church did step forward and took a bold posture. The moment demanded it. For the longest time it seemed that the South African nation was drowning in a sea of corruption and incompetence. It appeared as though the country's leaders and decision makers were not only responding to the crisis with a confusing ambivalence, but also seemed to be bedridden from a paralysing inertia that inexplicably prevented them from moving forward decisively regarding the acts of blatant greed and corruption that was being revealed to the South African nation on an almost daily basis. Unrepentant looters demanded to know from a robbed nation on the edge of an economic abyss what it was that they, the looters, had done wrong.

In my previous work I referred to a quote from an influential mega church leader in the USA, now retired.[27] To me, it remains one of the more inspirational sayings that I have heard from a church leader and I believe it is worth repeating here, 'The local church is the hope of the world and the positive impact of the work being done by church leaders far outweighs the impact of the contributions made by leaders in other spheres, including business and political leaders. Unlike leaders in business, government and the education sector, church leaders actually have the power to change the world.' This author remains persuaded that the Church of our Lord Jesus Christ can demonstrate this power, not through our own strength alone, but by remaining aware that our power comes from God, who increases the power of the weak and renews the strength of those who put their hope in the Lord. [28]

*'The causes which destroyed the ancient republics were numerous; but in Rome, one principal cause was the vast inequality of fortunes.'*

**Noah Webster**

# 9

## An End to Poverty?

*'You will always have the poor amongst you...'*

Matthew 26:11a (NLT)

During the year 2005, Professor Jeffrey Sachs published a book entitled, *The end of poverty*[29] with the subtitle, *how we can make it happen in our lifetime*. Within the pages of that work, the good professor outlines a 20 year plan up to the year 2025 on how extreme poverty can be eradicated in our own lifetime. He argues and points out how this united global effort, if carried out, will come at a fraction of the cost of doing little or nothing. This author found some of the professor's arguments rather persuasive, although we might now all have to concede that, nowhere within the pages of that book does the author foresee that the new enemy called COVID-19 would pay humankind a visit before the end of the year 2019.

I believe most will agree that the global commitment to end poverty was not very evident before the destructive pandemic made its unwelcome appearance and wreaked havoc on the world's economies and health systems. And whatever grand plans and good intentions to eradicate extreme poverty may still have been in place at the end of the year 2019, now lie in ruins. If the proposals and implementation models suggested by Sachs were indeed practical and doable, then clearly the poor of the planet have been on the receiving end of empty rhetoric and have again placed their hopes on leaders with low commitment to alleviate the plight of the world's most vulnerable communities.

All over the world hundreds of thousands of great, average and underperforming businesses have all folded together, leaving in their wake millions of newly unemployed people joining the ranks of the world's already unemployed persons. In some countries, the number of unemployed now outnumber the number of employed individuals. This, in turn, has led to a growing crisis of hunger and a significant threat to food security. The domino effect is increased social disintegration as people turn to illegal means to make ends meet and to ensure their survival. Petty crime increases, as well as more serious crimes which puts increased pressure on the systems of the state.

How far and how safe can humanity's ship sail on a sea of poverty? How sustainable is a world where one percent of the world's population continue to own more than fifty percent of the world's wealth? If the endless inertia is anything to go by, then it appears as though the wealthy of the world have long ago decided that they will be able to deal with any potential threat from the poor. Perhaps the wealthy, through their own active participation or even their absent silence, have observed that no matter how many times and in how many ways and places the peasants revolt, every time their efforts are easily suppressed by superior forces and then business always continues as usual. No problem.

Already in 2005, the good professor told us that we can do this - end poverty in our own lifetime. And that the cost of doing it would be negligible. In 2020, Bill Gates comes along and bemoans the fact that all the good work of the last 15 years has been dealt a severe, if not fatal, blow by the arrival of the new enemy at the gate. This is where the world finds itself right now. In the middle of a war - a different kind of war. One that is demanding all our energy and attention. It appears as if the old enemy of inequality will be left unchecked for another season as we exhaust ourselves through our efforts of using all our time and resources to prevent this new enemy, COVID-19, of completely breaking down the gate and taking complete control of the house of humanity.

*'The big thing standing in the way of that progress right now, is the pandemic ... we have been set back about 25 years in about 25 weeks.'*

**Goalkeepers Report – Bill & Melinda Gates Foundation**

# 10

# COVID-19 - The New Enemy

*'But no one can enter a strong man's house and plunder his goods, unless he first binds the strong man. Then indeed he may plunder his house.'*

Mark 3:27 (ESV)

COVID-19 arrived at the gate towards the end of 2019. It might emerge that, in future, the number 19 might illicit even more fear than the number 13. But be that as it may, the arrival of this new enemy of humanity was both unexpected and unwelcome. Never in our wildest nightmares could we have imagined that we would have to give up our way of life and our hard-fought freedoms in this manner. The freedom to leave our homes, move and travel where we wished, the freedom to watch a movie at the cinema of our choice, go for a haircut, visit our favourite restaurant or even just visit friends and family - all gone in one foul breath of the novel coronavirus.

The world as we knew it up to March 2020, was locked down overnight, destroying economies and livelihoods. All of this, so that we may be protected against this new evil. At the time of writing, more than 35 million people in the world had already been infected and the virus had already killed more than one million people on the planet. There are those who predict that before the year 2020 is over, we will witness more than double the present number (about another million) of deaths due to this new evil called COVID-19. The coming northern winter will apparently provide a conducive environment for the novel coronavirus to do its work. It is unbelievable that during the meeting of the WEF back in January 2020[30], this threat was not yet an item on the global agenda.

At the end of January 2020, it seemed that China was the only country in the world where COVID-19 deaths, due to the novel coronavirus, were recorded - a Chinese problem, in a manner of speaking. To the best of our knowledge, the first death outside of China was recorded in the Philippines during the first week of February 2020[31]. According to the World Health Organisation (WHO)[32], the highest number of daily deaths recorded back then was 108 people who died in China over a 24-hour period from 10 to 11 February 2020. Up to mid-February, this was the highest number of COVID-19 deaths for a single day. Then everything changed. Since then, this daily figure sometimes exceeded multiple thousands of deaths in a single day. COVID-19 is now one of our biggest global problems.

The threat of this novel coronavirus is very real. As has already been proven, responding to the enemy at the gate as simply a hoax, will have fatal consequences. It is regrettable that so many have dismissed the disease as a conspiracy and that they have been able to influence so many to ignore the maintaining of a safe social distance, wearing a mask and sanitising hands with greater care. Then, on the other hand, it may be regarded as equally naive when people allow themselves to be overcome with fear and hardly move out of their homes, including those who by the grace of God, are enjoying good health. When devoted church-going folk are persuaded to hide indoors and not darken the door of a church again, then perhaps other more sinister forces are at work.

I am not sure whether the Church of our Lord Jesus Christ has reflected long and hard enough on this new enemy at the gate. It is through this enemy that the biblically mandated gathering of the saints was relegated by political and other powers to a social event that is equal to a sports event or a rock concert. The same enemy that brought a crippling collapse to the health and economic systems of the world, has brought similar catastrophic effects right to the door and into the Church of Jesus Christ. Truth be told, when the new enemy showed up at the gate, it could not be foreseen that the doors of hope would be completely shut for many who were desperately in need of that hope, encouragement and care.

*'Inequality is a poison that is destroying livelihoods, stripping families of their dignity and splitting communities.'*

**Sharon Burrow**

# 11

## COVID-19 Conspiracies

*"What is truth?" Pilate asked...'*

John 18:38a (NLT)

What really happened in Wuhan?

There are those who refer to the novel coronavirus as something that was made in China. The supporters of this school of thought openly declare their suspicions about why, in the country where it all started, with more than a billion people, less than 5 000 of China's citizens have succumbed to the COVID-19 disease that went on to kill more than a million world citizens to date. And the members of this school of suspicion are not only suspicious about how it all started, they continually draw our attention to the fact that since the middle of April 2020 no one has died from the virus in China, while people all over the world continue to die from this disease that was manufactured in China.

As mentioned in a previous chapter, on 12 January 2017, at the Georgetown University Forum[33], speaking on the topic, 'Pandemic Preparedness in the Next Administration' / 'Global Health Experts Advise Advance Planning for Inevitable Pandemic', Dr Anthony Fauci warned that, in addition to both ongoing and new diseases, the new administration (the Trump administration) should, without a doubt, expect a surprise outbreak. There are many who find this prediction too much of a coincidence in the light of the COVID-19 pandemic that sprang its surprise during the fourth year of the Trump administration.

It is no small wonder that when ordinary people become aware that decisions are made in dark corners where they cannot see and that the rich and powerful grab opportunities long before news agencies and the masses even hear about it, it is not at all difficult for them to take the short next step of giving more serious attention to the almost uncountable number of conspiracy theories that have come to light, particularly during the first months of COVID-19. In the book *Animal Farm*[34], the pigs maintained that they were more equal than the other animals. Access to information is another aspect where enormous inequalities are perpetuated in a world where some insist that they are more equal than others.

It is to these two coronavirus conspiracies above that we now turn our closer attention without attaching any intellectual weight to the veracity or gravity of these so-called conspiracies, except for the fact that they are out there and probably worth noting. In this regard, we will limit our examination to the specific comments that have already been mentioned earlier on. I am referring here to the predictions of the billionaire Bill Gates and Dr Anthony Fauci, as these may probably be the most noteworthy of the lot. On a cautionary note, with all the technology that is currently available to manipulate pictures, words and voices, it must be kept in mind that one can never be quite sure whether what one sees and hears is the real thing.

On closer examination of the content of the two speeches made by Gates and Fauci during January 2017, it becomes evident that the two gentlemen have made those statements within the broader context of historical outbreaks and the fact that they may reoccur soon. In my opinion, there is nothing unusual there. What appears to have been good food for conspiracy theorists is Fauci's choice of the word 'surprise', but then he curiously provides the specific time frame which plays out exactly within the four-year period of his prediction. Even a less suspicious individual like myself is left wondering - what kind of a surprise is that?

*'There should exist amongst the citizens neither extreme poverty nor excessive wealth for both are productive of great evil.'*

**Plato**

# 12

## Inequality - The Old Enemy

*'Do nothing out of selfish ambition or vain conceit. Rather, in humility value others above yourselves...'*

Philippians 2;3 (NIV)

Inequality is an ancient enemy that has been living comfortably alongside the inhabitants of planet earth since time immemorial. This enemy operates way beyond the realm of race and class, and has demonstrated its ease of access into the most corrupt environments where there is no evidence of respect for the poor, women and children, the aged, the disabled, the sick and all other vulnerable members of society. This becomes clear when those who claim to have delivered others from the hand of their former oppressors, now openly defend their acts of corruption and nepotism as quite in order.

During the year 2020, those on the receiving end of the effects of global inequality have again faced the perennial truth that when the days are dark, the friends are few. They could only follow in the news media how the privileged few were gaining access to opportunities that were never made available to those who also had the right of access to those opportunities. Once again, ease of access would be determined by one's connections and one's proximity to the dark corners where access would be discussed and determined. It is almost a certainty that an individual or organisation will benefit not really because of competence, capacity or the ability to deliver, but by being connected, however incompetent or unsuitable for the project or assignment that individual or organisation may be.

What is it that makes humankind so tolerant of this age-old enemy? It might be useful to gain some insights from the previously mentioned article edited by Mitch Brown entitled, 'The Inequality Paradox, Inequality Awareness, and System Justification', written by Carmen Cervone & Andrea Scatolon.[35] The conclusion that the writers come to is that generally, nothing is being done to fight inequality. As indicated in an earlier chapter, like me, those authors also wonder aloud why there is no collective struggle towards greater equality, just as there is for other issues such as climate change or equal rights? For our benefit they went further and provided us with some reasons and explanations why the enemy of inequality has been tolerated for so many generations before us.

Like with most academic studies, the writers of the article suggest a degree of complexity regarding the generational prevalence of inequality in our world. According to the learned authors there is no straightforward answer to the question why nothing is done about inequality. To use their own words the answer is 'neither easy nor certain'. To begin with, inequality might be preferred by people (wished for). It is also possible that inequality may be perceived as fair, because there are certain characteristics that lead some people to deserve more and others to deserve less. Amongst other reasons offered by the authors is the fact that there is a severe underestimation of economic inequality across the globe and that inequality is justified through the stereotyping of people.

The authors conclude that the following paradox exists. It seems that while many reject high economic disparities, they also believe that nothing is wrong with the status quo and that society is fair. Despite the above conclusion, the compilers of the article encourage us that the historical data tells us that there is reason for hope. In my humble opinion, if the one 26-

word sentence containing the data is removed from the 5000-word article, there are few, if any, signs of hope to be found in the rest of the document. But it is perhaps based on this kind of hope that world leaders and organisations continue to design plans that have, as its aim, the significant reduction of the stubborn inequality gap which has become as perennial as the grass.

*'It is important to note that innovation and growth in itself is not enough and not sufficient to moderate inequality of wealth.'*

**Thomas Piketty**

# 13

## Paralysis by Analysis

*'You can make many plans, but the Lord's purpose will prevail.'*

Proverbs 19:21 (NLT)

Plans, plans, plans.

Every time world leaders come up with a new plan or they simply relaunch the old plan.

Having no regard for the reasons of the failure of all the previous plans, more money is invested into the design of a new one. But there is very little evidence of any follow through or any effort to implement those loudly laid plans. It is always more rhetoric than action. It seems that we have mastered the art of talk and have almost entirely lost our capacity and ability to implement anything good and lasting. The words are always there, but the commitment and follow through is mostly lacking. It appears the political will to do all the right things at the right time is just not there. We write policy after policy, amending them and replacing them with new ideas and new plans. It appears as if it is going around in circles with seemingly no destination or desire to reach such destination.

When the secretary-general of the United Nations, António Guterres, delivered his speech at the Nelson Mandela Annual Lecture 2020 on 18 July 2020, he made several references to documents and plans that aim to deal with the inequalities that exist on planet earth. In the earlier part of his speech he referred to the 2030 Agenda for Sustainable Development, the Paris Agreement as well as the Addis Ababa Action Agenda. Towards the end of his delivery, he alluded to the Roadmap for Digital Cooperation and Giga, an ambitious project to get every school in the world online.[36] The good secretary-general also highlights a significant number of the prevailing global inequalities.

After making his audience aware of the fact that we face the deepest global recession since World War II, and the broadest collapse in incomes since 1870, the UN representative went on to mention the many inequalities that must be confronted. During his speech, António Guterres warned that we should not only be concerned about income and wealth inequality, but that factors like gender, family and ethnic background, race, whether people have a disability, and other inequalities also come into the equation. Inequalities exist as far as basic human rights, to which we are all entitled, are concerned, like access to food, healthcare, water and sanitation, education, decent work, justice and social security.

It is not an exaggeration to say that in South Africa there is no shortage of plans. And in addition to that we seem to have also mastered the art of replacing the one plan with another, with little or no evidence on the implementation front. During 1994 there was the Reconstruction and Development Plan (RDP) followed by the Growth, Employment And Redistribution plan (GEAR) in 1996, only to be followed nine years later by yet another plan called the Accelerated And Shared Growth Initiative for South Africa (ASGISA) - in 2010 there was the New Growth Plan (NGP). As if all these plans were not enough the next one launched in 2013 would be "re-launched" in 2017!

During 2013, the South African government launched a 17-year plan towards the year 2030. Four years later (2017) a relaunch and rebrand of sorts was announced, dubbed a new call to action. The document contains all the appropriate phrases and all the correct language that one would expect in a so-called National Development Plan (NDP).[37] Amongst other, the plan contains an almost unbelievably ambitious aim to eliminate poverty and a more realistic aim to reduce inequality by 2030. The plan speaks of an inclusive economy, enhancing the capacity of the state, promoting leadership and partnerships and drawing on the energies of the South African people.

Many other plans are made and either forgotten or abandoned. New plans are designed, or old ones redesigned. Often very grand and lofty plans, but with little will to see them through to their conclusion with little or no evidence of a genuine intent to implement. The latest South African plan is our Economic Recovery Plan[38], on top of all the other plans.

*'Can one preach at home inequality of races and nations and advocate abroad goodwill towards all men?'*

**Dorothy Thompson**

# 14

## The Scoreboard

*'But don't begin until you count the cost. For who would begin construction of a building without first calculating the cost to see if there is enough money to finish it?'*

Luke 14:28 (NLT)

About three years ago the Bill & Belinda Gates Foundation established an organisation called Goalkeepers (referred to in previous chapters). The organisation publishes an annual report, the 'Goalkeepers Report', which tracks the progress toward the Sustainable Development Goals (SDGs). The United Nations outlined 17 so-called global goals in 2015. It is an ambitious list that hopes to achieve prosperity for everyone by the year 2030. These global goals are in fact the Sustainable Development Goals (SDGs) of which Goalkeepers are keeping score.[39]

The goals include ending poverty, eradicating hunger, securing good health and wellbeing, quality education, gender equality, access to clean water and sanitation, affordable and cleaner energy, decent work and economic growth, industry innovation and infrastructure, end inequality, develop sustainable cities and communities, foster responsible consumption and production, take climate action seriously, keeping in mind life on land and below the water as well as justice for all. These goals will ostensibly be achieved through global partnership, and international cooperation and collaboration will, therefore, be essential.

South Africa has a somewhat different set of goals, published a few years before the United Nation's Sustainable Development Goals. The National Development Plan or NDP[40] for short, is a plan to unite South Africans, unleash the energies of its citizens, grow an inclusive economy, build capabilities, and enhance the capability of the state and leaders working together to solve complex problems. South Africa's list includes nation building, social cohesion, inclusive social protection, safety and freedom from fear, healthcare for all, economic growth and employment, a skilled workforce, vibrant rural communities, sustainable human settlements, accountable local government, an efficient public service and a natural environment.

Interestingly enough, the South African list emerged after a process of significant public participation which ended up with a commission producing a diagnostic report which identified (besides some achievements) nine shortcomings in the nation, namely high unemployment, the skewed quality of school education, poor infrastructure, inadequate and under-maintained spatial divides which hobble inclusive development. The report also found that the South African economy is unsustainably resource-intensive, the public health system cannot meet demand or sustain quality, public services are uneven and often of poor quality, corruption levels are high and South Africa remains a divided society.

The reason for providing all the above detail is to demonstrate two things. One, everybody seems to know what the problems are in our world and two, the reality of inequality in our world is revealed in almost all the basic aspects of everyday life like having a decent job, a decent place to live, food on the table and having unproblematic access to things like good education and healthcare. The question is, how are we doing on the commitment and implementation side? What is the scoreboard telling us? Is humanity winning or losing? Do we have the will to win? Do we want to win? But that would be score keeping, not goalkeeping. So, the real question is, what are the goalkeepers doing?

In the game of soccer, a goalkeeper is someone who protects the net so that the opponents are prevented from getting the ball past the post and into the net. Are we willing to protect the net against the two evil twins of COVID-19 and inequality? Or are we perhaps being discouraged by the scoreboard? Is winning no longer an option?

*'Washing one's hands off the conflict between the powerful and powerless means to side with the powerful, not to be neutral.'*

**Paolo Freire**

# 15

## A Few Good People

> *'But the Lord told Gideon, "There are still too many! Bring them down to the spring, and I will test them to determine who will go with you and who will not."'*
>
> Judges 7:4 (NLT)

Margaret Mead said, 'Never doubt that a small group of thoughtful, committed, citizens can change the world. Indeed, it is the only thing that ever has.'[41] In the seventh chapter of the biblical book of Judges, there is the story of Gideon who received instruction from God to eventually reduce his army from 32 000 to 300 men. God also provided His reason to Gideon for the instruction. After achieving the victory over the enemy, he (Gideon) and his people might boast that they won a battle on their own strength. As the story goes, in the end, the battle was won without anyone having done much more than lift a finger. The story reminds me of the words of Paul in the fourth chapter of his second letter to the Corinthians where he reminds them that the all-surpassing power comes from God and not from us.[42]

All over the world, for the longest time, it seems that when people come into positions of power, barring the few exceptions, they end up abusing the power of the office that gave them the power in the first place. When this abuse of power takes full effect, it is usually followed by the abuse of the rights of the powerless and the voiceless. As we have learnt the hard way, when this power starts to corrupt people it ends up corrupting them absolutely. Election after election, the powerful run their political campaigns in the name of the powerless and the voiceless, making them the same promises repeatedly and the masses vote them into power again and again. These unequal power relations have been with humanity since time immemorial.

As in some other countries, especially in South Africa, there is a call to action. What is very encouraging is the recent prominence of the Church in this regard. After maintaining what this author would call a low profile during the earlier part of the pandemic, it seemed the Church was jerked into action by the blatant corruption that was exposed during the southern winter of 2020. Many voices have been heard calling for the citizenry to revolt against the corrupt and evil system led by unapologetic politicians who cannot seem to understand what all the fuss is about. One would love to say the exceptions aside, but who are really the "exceptions" when the unrepentant transgressors just seem to continue unashamed on their path of greed and corruption amidst the silence of their colleagues?

As was the case with Gideon and his small band of followers, even now, at the present time and under current conditions, it might take only a few good people to make the difference. In my earlier work, I referred to Nehemiah and his efforts to rebuild the wall in Jerusalem.[43] How each one was working on the wall near or opposite his or her own house. Each one of us, in our own small corner of the world, can make our contribution towards making our communities, cities and countries a better environment to live and work in. We should not underestimate what results our increased, accelerated efforts may produce. In the end, we might all stand amazed at what a small group of thoughtful, committed citizens might bring to pass.

The keyword is commitment. It will be of great help if ever there can be a collective (global) view that the evil twins at the gate are indeed the enemies of humankind. This will be a necessity before we will be willing to act against them. Once we can agree that the combined effect from this lethal collaboration is a threat to all our futures, then it should not be too difficult to also agree that more than lip service will be required to launch a sustainable offensive against the evil pair.

*'If there was a wrong, if there is a lack of justice and there is an inequality, then someone needs to say something.
And why not me?'*

**Megan Markle**

# 16

## The Time is Right

*'...you did not recognise the time of your visitation.'*

Luke 19:44b (NASB)

Ancient words. Voices from the past. Encouraging us.

Warning us. Cautioning us. Prompting us to appreciate the hour that is thrust upon us.

William Shakespeare warned us, 'There is a tide in the affairs of men, which taken at the flood, leads on to fortune. Omitted, all the voyage of their life is bound in shallows and in miseries. On such a full sea are we now afloat. And we must take the current when it serves or lose our ventures.'[44] Then Margaret Mead came and encouraged us, 'Never doubt that a small group of thoughtful, committed, citizens can change the world. Indeed, it is the only thing that ever has.' More recently Martin Luther King (Jr.) reminded us that the time is always right to do the right thing. It is critically important to have the perspective of these individuals during these challenging and uncertain times.

The hour is calling out for our collective response - locally and globally. As António Guterres, the secretary-general of the United Nations has articulated it, 'we belong to each other… we stand together, or we fall apart… now is the time for global leaders to decide.' Guterres advocates a new global deal, based on fair globalisation, on the rights and dignity of every human being and in which the developing world has a much stronger voice in global decision making. And it would perhaps stand us all in good stead if we heed the final warning of the good secretary-general at the end of his speech on 18 July 2020 during the Nelson Mandela Annual Lecture, 'we are at breaking point'.

It is this author's very strong conviction that, in the end, when we look back, or even later when the history of our time is written, it might be revealed that there were many historical moments that were not maximised because we did not respond appropriately when history offered our generation the opportunity. Very often, these historical moments carry within them both agony and opportunity. It could easily happen that we become so overwhelmed by the trauma of the time, that we find ourselves semi paralysed into a continuous and almost permanent state of mental inertia. There is a school of thought that encourages us to live in the moment. Perhaps the idea deserves more of our attention, because living in the moment might help us to respond responsibly and appropriately.

To quote The Bard again, 'On such a full sea are we now afloat.' The lethal collaborative partnership between the evil twins of COVID-19 and inequality has turned the tide against humanity in more ways than one. The voyage has been made much more dangerous, and the ships of almost all the nations of the world are now being threatened by even greater swells, on a more dangerous sea, in a stormy night where no stars are visible. As one of South Africa's well-known former church leaders once remarked, 'Those of us in the more favourable position should not fool ourselves that we will be able to sail safely on a sea of poverty and inequality'.

If such is the time and these are the conditions that continue to prevail, is an uncritical silence really an appropriate response to the moment we are in? As George Santayana reminded those of us who tend to forget, 'Those who cannot remember the past are condemned to repeat it.' For many generations, the threat from our old enemy of worldwide economic inequality has been left almost unattended. Hopefully, since our new enemy, who has joined him at the gate, has again focused our attention on the very real threat to humankind, what will be our collective response, that the good secretary-general of the United Nations has called for, be? And even if a full and complete collective response is unattainable, where is that small group of thoughtful, committed, citizens who can change the world?

*'Certainly, the poverty, the discrimination, the episodic unemployment could not but strike an inquiring youngster: why did these exist, and what could we do about them.'*

**Joseph E. Stiglitz**

# 17

## Re-imagining the Future

> *'In the future, the mountain with the Lord's temple will be the highest of all. It will reach above the hills; every nation will rush to it.'*
>
> Isaiah 2:2 (CEV)

The new normal. Life will probably never be the same again.

Almost everyone is telling us that we will simply have to get used to this. The realities of the new normal will be a daily part of our immediate futures. Over the next year or two, very little is expected to change as far as our new lifestyle is concerned. That is a life of maintaining a safe social distance, the regular sanitising of hands, equipment, utensils and devices, as well as the continued wearing of protective masks. Should we not take this seriously, the threat of a second wave of devastation could prove even more deadly than the first. The lessons from the first wave (which continue to be learnt on an almost daily basis) should not be taken lightly or be easily forgotten.

Lest we forget, even during the good old days, before the disruption caused by COVID-19, the global community was potently unable to deal with the challenges and consequences related to the worldwide phenomenon of inequality. The unequal power relations, race relations and gender relations that existed on the planet were fully exposed under the stark light of the pandemic caused by the novel coronavirus. And now that the economy of almost every country in the world has shrunk to a fraction of its previous size, the possibilities of effectively dealing with the scourge of inequality has been dealt a severe blow. Everywhere politicians and other world leaders have learnt the new art of hiding behind the impact of COVID-19 while imposing conflicting and confusing rules on people.

Today, 29 September 2020, for the first time in seven months, I am taking a two-hour domestic flight to another city. The buzz of people at the airport is gone. It appears almost deserted. Most of the shops are still closed. Only here and there some brave entrepreneur is continuing with business. The business class lounges are closed. No more relaxing and enjoying free refreshments before the flight. No more shoeshine man. New protocols are in place. One must complete and sign a declaration that you show no symptoms of fever or difficulty breathing, that you have not been in contact with certain persons and that you have not been attending social gatherings of more than 50 people. There are hand sanitising stations around almost every corner and one must walk longer distances after parking your vehicle or after being dropped off at the Airport.

The founder of the World Economic Forum (WEF), Klaus Schwab, has coined a new phrase, 'the great reset'. Yes, our entire world has been reset and will henceforth continue on a path that will be very different from the one we have trod before Christmas last year. As if the million people that have already died because of the microscopic virus, that has brought the world to its knees, is not enough, we are warned that things are bound to get worse before they get better. Some experts warn that we should expect twice or even three times that number of deaths by the end of the last quarter of 2020. The number of unemployed continue to climb and thousands of highly qualified graduates and professionals are joining their ranks. In the end, what effect will the "great reset" have on the gains of the last decade, like the billion or more people who in recent years, have been moved out of extreme poverty?

Uncertainty and fear will probably form a prominent part of our lives for some time to come. And even if that is probably not the ideal way one should live one's life, there are clearly some aspects that will be non-negotiable, like living our daily lives taking greater care of ourselves and living more responsibly and going about our business with greater caution. The wearing of masks, the maintaining of safe social distances and the sanitising of hands and surfaces is a very real part of the new normal. Even when we reach Level 0 and large sports gatherings and concerts can take place, will the crowds return? And if the longing for such social activity bring people back to these events, how much time will it take before we fall back into the old normal, at great risk to ourselves?

And what about the Church of our Lord Jesus Christ? As Dr Bruce Theron puts it, 'We are left wondering how the work, witness and ministry of the Church will look in a post COVID-19 world.'[45] Having been relegated to the level of a so-called social gathering during the greater part of the year 2020, the Church has been on the receiving end of unequal treatment by the powers that be. My return flight home from the city of Johannesburg, is no less packed than my flight out the previous day. We are sitting shoulder to shoulder with frequent accidental physical contact. What kind of logic is this? For what good reason should one maintain a safe social distance of one and half metres in church, but in an airplane there are no such risks? What is the explanation for such unequal treatment? And why is the Church not demanding a reason? What is really going on here?

I am aware that there are those who would offer a view that through all this, the Church has not exactly been quietly licking her wounds in the corner. That indeed, she (the Church) has been all over the place. There has been so much online activity. So many calls to prayer. So many webinars and seminars. Online conferences and engagements, so many good news stories from all over. About foot soldiers of our Lord Jesus Christ everywhere, who continue to do their daily Christian duty of making their world a better place. And God forbid that we suspend all the important work that is being done currently. This should continue. The Church cannot afford to stop and do nothing. There is too much at stake and the work is too important for us to come down and deal with the Sanballats and Tobiahs.[46]

But have we done enough?

*'It's well proven that if you have equality in society, society flourishes and if you have inequality it doesn't. So, it's good for everybody.'*

**Sandra Gavran**

# 18

## A Better World

*'No eye has seen, no ear has heard, and no mind has imagined what God has prepared for those who love him.'*

1 Corinthians 2:9 (NLT)

We are working towards a better world. So we say.

So many organisations striving towards the same goal. And so many billions have been raised in the name of the poor.

There are so many great organisations doing wonderful work across the world, including on our own continent and in our own country, South Africa. Led and driven by individuals who believe in the future and a better world for all of us to live in, they continue to make a real difference in the lives of so many people despite of all the corruption and mismanagement that is going on in the countries where they are. Then, on the other hand there are those (almost fatalistic) detractors who are wondering aloud whether all these efforts are mere attempts at rearranging the deck chairs on a sinking Titanic. Perhaps this pessimistic view deserves a little more attention.

I am reminded of a line from the poem 'Desiderata' written by the American, Max Ehrmann, published around 1927[47], 'keep interested in your own career, however humble; it is a real possession in the changing fortunes of time.' It so happens that, about a quarter century ago, I was enjoying accelerating upward mobility in the corporate world. It was during the infancy of South Africa's new democracy. Those glorious, unforgettable years of the late President Nelson Mandela's era. In my sixty years, I cannot recall a time before or after in the history of our nation, when such a period of optimism and faith in our collective future as a nation, existed.

On the wall in my study hangs a photograph of a group of young business professionals (most of us in our early and mid-thirties), some remaining evidence of the dream of South Africa's rainbow nation, now perhaps no more than a distant, sometimes ridiculed, discredited memory. In my opinion, unfairly so. Because whatever the shortcomings and imperfections of that dream, history has judged the Madiba years far more favourably than the time of the capture of the South African state or the many false starts to the nation's so-called new dawn. During those last few years of the previous millennium, everywhere in the world where I was fortunate to travel, I was welcomed with big smiles and open arms as one of Madiba's people. As I have already said, those were glorious days.

As the twentieth century ended, I became aware of an overwhelming sense of urgency, that although the business world and the corporate ladder was beckoning, it was time for me to leave in response to a different calling. One that was beginning to consume my entire being, and it was becoming in the words of the biblical prophet, Jeremiah, 'like a fire in my bones'.[48] By that time, I had already been an ordained minister in my denomination for quite a few years, and so accepted a full-time call to a church in one of Cape Town's poorer neighbourhoods, where I am still in active ministry. From there I went on to become involved in a number of city, continental and international organisations (movements, really) that work towards making the world a better place.

This, then, (with acknowledgement to Max Ehrmann) has been my humble career over the last twenty years, and one that I can only describe as the most fulfilling, most rewarding period of my entire lifetime so far. In this regard, I am most grateful that I have been blessed with the privilege and good fortune to have worked with, and continue to work alongside, some of the most amazing city and world changers of this generation. It is my prayer that the work of these organisations would continue, even at an accelerated pace and that what they do and the impact that they are making in the world, would be even more recognised and celebrated than before.

But it is also my prayer that all the sacrifice and effort of these organisations, movements and individuals will not be lost because there was no global, collective effort to deal with the two enemies at the gate.

*'Poverty is not an accident. Like slavery and apartheid, it is man-made and can be removed by the actions of human beings.'*

**Nelson Mandela**

# 19

## An Opportunity for the Church

*'But the time is coming - indeed it's here now - when true worshippers will worship the Father in spirit and in truth. The Father is looking for those who will worship him that way.'*

John 4:23 (NLT)

An hour has been thrust upon the world.

Our Lord Jesus Christ himself warned the citizens of Jerusalem[49] what may happen when one does not recognise the hour of your visitation. At the present time, it could be argued that an hour has arrived that warns all the citizens of the world about the ineffectiveness of the continued use of empty clichés and sound bites. It is an hour that screams for responsible action. In an Old Testament story in the Bible, a similar caution was issued to Esther[50] when her own uncle warned her, 'If you keep quiet at a time like this, deliverance and relief for the Jews will arise from some other place, but you and your relatives will die. Who knows if perhaps you were made queen for just such a time as this?'

In the end, the Church of our Lord Jesus Christ can never be free from the burden of responsibility to be an active partner in the management and maintenance of our planet earth. This role and responsibility are not only based on Scripture, but a God given mandate. In this regard, it is probably fair to say that it will not be possible for the Church to do this alone. On the contrary, for the longest time now, quite the opposite has been the reality in our world. The Church, whether due to her own dereliction of duty or through marginalisation by forces more powerful than herself, has found herself on the sidelines, especially during this crisis that was brought about by the deadly novel coronavirus.

For many within the Body of our Lord Jesus Christ, any greater participation in the management of the planet and its resources may require a brave revisit to our own theology. It will be near impossible to become and remain involved as a partner in the management and maintenance of our planet if there remains a reluctance to accept the essential requirement of collaboration with those who may not share our theology. The taking of hands and sharing of resources is paramount as far as the implementation of the corrective processes to care for the world's citizens and the environments where they live, walk and work, is concerned.

This author is aware of wonderful work that is being done across the globe through existing partnerships and collaboration between religious, civic, business and other organisations. Perhaps these efforts have been under reported, under advertised and under celebrated. Maybe the reason why there is little or no awareness about the impact of these endeavours is because they are underestimated, underrated and undervalued. Besides collaborative efforts, there are also the focused interventions of many parachurch organisations doing amazing work, especially across the African continent. These include, amongst other initiatives, Farming God's Way and African Orchard.

In my earlier work, I have highlighted the important relief work carried out by the Church during the first three months of the worldwide lockdown period. I am confident that history will judge the response of the Body of Christ in the hour of crisis with kindness and appreciation. When the early threat of food security hit the poorest households, the Church did what she was called to do - she was there for the orphan, the widow and the stranger. But while the Church was carrying out that very essential duty, many leaders in secular authority were doing quite the opposite. While the Church was feeding and clothing the needy, many injustices were being carried out, including the misappropriation of funds that were, in fact, earmarked for the very type of relief being carried out by the Church.

I am not sure whether history will judge us kindly if we do not respond decisively to these injustices, particularly those in our own house. As Alan Platt, the global leader of the City Changers movement warned us, 'if the Church does not deal with its own challenges first, it will become very difficult for the Church to make any meaningful impact outside of the church walls.'

It seems that there is so much left to do and that so far, until now, so little has been done.

*'Today in many places we hear a call for greater security. But until exclusion and inequality in society and between peoples is reversed, it will be impossible to eliminate violence.'*

**Pope Francis**

# 20

## Doing the Right Thing

*'For I was hungry and you gave me something to eat, I was thirsty and you gave me something to drink, I was a stranger and you invited me in, I needed clothes and you clothed me, I was sick and you looked after me, I was in prison and you came to visit me.'*

Matthew 25:35-36 (NIV)

Dr Martin Luther King (Jr.) said the time is always right to do the right thing. Is it right for us to continue ignoring the threat of the evil twins at the gate, especially our old enemy of inequality? But perhaps we are getting ahead of ourselves with that question. Maybe we should first ask a different question - what would Jesus do? And if we were to start searching anywhere for the answer to that question, what better place than to take our search to the Gospels of the New Testament. Because it is only when we retrace the earthly steps of the leader of the Church, that we find that they lead to wherever and whatever the need was, whether hunger, sickness or injustice.

The gospels leave us with no doubt that our Lord Jesus Christ had a consistent and deep-rooted empathy with the marginalised and the vulnerable of His day. According to Matthew's gospel, 'when he saw the crowds, he had compassion on them, because they were harassed and helpless, like sheep without a shepherd.'[51] Jesus made special effort and time for all those who endured affliction, including those who suffered from the dreaded disease of leprosy and He was even labelled a friend of sinners, a wine bibber and a glutton. When observing the injustices being perpetrated in the temple precinct, He rebuked the money changers, accusing them of turning God's house into a den of robbers.

In the New Testament book of Acts, there is clear indication that the first generation of Christians continued with what they observed in the life and ministry of their leader. They showed genuine interest and concern for the poor amongst them, to the extent that some of them would, from time to time, liquidate their assets and then distribute the proceeds amongst the needy. They took view that none of their possessions was their own, but they shared everything they had.[52] As a result of this camaraderie and solidarity, there were no needy persons amongst them. Similarly, they often took a stand against those in power and declared that they would prefer to obey God rather than human beings.[53]

When one has regard for the further history of the early Church, beyond the book of Acts, even into the second and third centuries of the Roman era, we find that this human solidarity and collective concern continued amongst the followers of our Lord Jesus Christ.
During a devastating epidemic[54], because the early believers did not fear death, at great risk to themselves, they went out of their way to provide basic care to the sick and dying rather than abandon them. Through simple gestures like providing food and water for those who were too weak to help themselves, hundreds, if not thousands, of lives were saved. They did not only provide this courageous care to only their own circle, but to all the afflicted.

Very often, when the odds seem insurmountable, we decide to not even try. Why pursue an assignment that is doomed to failure? Yet, we also know that it has been proven over and again that success and failure have a lot to do with attitude - the can-do attitude. And whether we will be able to pull it off or not, is less important than the question that has been asked - what is the right thing to do? Should we allow these evil twins to enter at will and destroy what is left of the planet? God forbids! That would be a blatant dereliction of our God given duty to take responsibility for the planet and all its resources, including the human resources.[55] Why are we going to such great lengths to deal with only one of the twins and ignoring the other?

*'The ultimate tragedy is not the oppression and cruelty by the bad people but the silence over that by the good people.'*

**Martin Luther King (Jr.)**

# 21

## How Will the Church Respond?

> *'I was a stranger and you did not take Me in, naked and you did not clothe Me, sick and in prison and you did not visit Me.'*
>
> Matthew 25:43 (NKJV)

Is COVID-19 really the new enemy that has joined our old enemy at the gate? Could it be that our arsenal was so inadequate that we could not decisively ward off this microscopic sized threat to our existence? Or, as the conspiracy theorists would have it, should we perhaps be cautious of a far greater and a far more dangerous enemy behind the disease, lurking somewhere in the shadows or perhaps even hiding in plain sight within our own walls? After all, how coincidental can it be that three years prior to the arrival of our new enemy, we were already warned about a surprise outbreak and an intentional outbreak that was to come? What kind of a surprise was that? And how many undeclared and unannounced surprises are still waiting for us up ahead?

At the end of my previous work, I asked the following two questions about the Church. Was the voice of the Church really heard during the devastation of the worldwide pandemic caused by the novel coronavirus, and did the Church really say what was needed to be said?[56] Historically, at least, errors and scandals aside, the Church cannot be accused of doing entirely nothing. The historical contributions and responses of the Church, when the hour demanded a contribution and a response, are too well recorded for them to be repeated here. Even now, and right through the pandemic, there are individuals and organisations everywhere making a difference as representatives of God and the Church.

Kindly allow me to make a few examples. There are the ongoing efforts to train and educate the existing, as well as the new generation of leaders in almost all aspects of life and ministry. Before and during the pandemic, especially parachurch organisations based all over the world have been equipping leaders to be better leaders, better managers, better stewards, better disciples, better organisers. Leaders are being sharpened how to pray more effectively, how to fast more effectively and how to reach their communities and cities more effectively. Organisations are teaching people to farm God's way, how to run their businesses God's way and ordinary believers are being trained how to impact their workplaces God's way.

All of this is going on while, around a "second table", the unequals meet after those, who are more equal than others, have already deliberated around a "first table" and determined how the less equals will be engaged, collaborated with and deployed in the name of the great change or the great reset or the great whatever. It must be understood that all these efforts require funding and this author is aware of many philanthropists, especially in the wealthy northern parts of the world, whose hands and hearts are wide open to fund these very novel endeavours of these parachurch organisations. But respectfully, in most cases, like the master of the vineyard, these benefactors choose exactly where and how their money will be spent.

Again, please grant this author another kindness. Believe me when I say that there is no judgement on my part about the way efforts on how to advance God's kingdom on earth are run and financed. Based on my travels and experiences, these are merely my honest observations of how things are being done for a long time, even now. And perhaps our Lord Jesus Christ has left us the story of the vineyard manager and the reference to the poor for posterity. Perhaps there are biblical lessons hidden in those two examples from the Gospels for us. But it is perhaps in our Lord's responses to the injustices of His own time, from which we may draw some important insights that may be of value to the Body of Christ as far as Her own responses to the current reality is concerned.

*'Not everything that is faced can be changed.
But nothing can be changed until it is faced.'*

**James Baldwin**

# Afterword

## What would Jesus do?

> '*Jesus made a whip from some ropes and chased them all out of the Temple. He drove out the sheep and cattle, scattered the money changers' coins over the floor, and turned over their tables.*'
>
> John 2:15 (NLT)

Two chapters ago and in my previous work, I described the leader of the movement called Christianity, as a man who had compassion for those who lived on the fringes of society, the downtrodden, the marginalised, and the outcasts of the human race. That his detractors referred to him as a wine bibber and a glutton, a friend of sinners.[57] That his short earthly life was marked by conflict with organised religion, to the point that he turned the tables of the money changers within the temple precinct. If our reflections are about the response of the Church, it might prove useful to revisit some of the lessons about our Lord Jesus Christ, as they have come down to us in the pages of the four Gospels of the New Testament.

Chris de Burgh's song of 1975, 'Just another poor boy', is about Jesus of Nazareth. This description of the earthly status of Jesus is probably not far from the truth, considering the circumstances surrounding his humble birth and the fact that when his life was under threat as an infant, his parents sought and found refuge in one of the poorest continents on the planet, namely Africa. In His later adult life, someone pledged to follow our Lord wherever He would go, and Jesus warned him that, 'the foxes have dens and the birds of the heavens have nests, but the Son of Man has no place to lay his head.'[58] In fact, His short early life was spent amongst the poor, the hungry, the sick and other forgotten and rejected people.

There are so many examples in the Gospel stories about the intentional efforts of our Lord Jesus Christ to, in His own words, 'seek and save the lost.'[59] He went out of his way to reach those on the outskirts, socialising with politically or religiously incorrect individuals, like tax collectors, women of ill repute and even touched those who were known to have contagious diseases. The person being described in the pages of the New Testament is clearly someone with a heart for the poverty stricken, often moved with compassion when He came face to face with the daily realities of their lives, because they almost always seemed 'confused and helpless, like sheep without a shepherd.'[60]

Jesus not only fed the hungry and healed the sick and demon possessed, His dealings with and responses to those in positions of political or religious authority are equally educational. Jesus referred to Herod as 'that fox'[61] and made it very clear to Pontius Pilate that Pilate had no authority over Him. In fact, our Lord told him in so many words, 'You would have no power over me at all unless it were given to you from above.'[62] Earlier in the same gospel (John), Jesus declared that no one could take His life from Him. That He was sacrificing it voluntarily. That He had the authority to lay His life down when He wanted to and to take it up again.[63]

What would Jesus do? In this time of reflection on an appropriate response by the Church to the current state of the globe, spending some time pondering about this question will probably stand us all in good stead. Whether we be world leaders who have consciously or unconsciously marginalised the Church by relegating Her to the status of just another social gathering. Or whether we be those on the inside, who have remained aloof and silent during a time when the situation has been crying out for our visible, audible presence and intervention. What would Jesus do?

Or perhaps the other question posed by Megan Markle is even more relevant, 'If there was a wrong, if there is a lack of justice and there is an inequality, then someone needs to say something. And why not me?'

# References

1. https://www.worldometers.info/coronavirus/

2. Herbert, Trevor, The Church, The City & The Virus, 2020

3. https://www.un.org/sg/en/content/sg/statement/2020-07-18/secretary-generals-nelson-mandela-lecture-%E2%80%9Ctackling-the-inequality-pandemic-new-social-contract-for-new-era%E2%80%9D-delivered

4. The World Economic Forum, based in Cologny, Geneva Canton, Switzerland, is an NGO, founded in 1971.

5. The United Nations is an intergovernmental organisation that aims to maintain international peace and security, develop friendly relations amongst nations, achieve international cooperation, and be a centre for harmonising the actions of nations.

6. https://www.in-mind.org/article/fair-enough-the-inequality-paradox-inequality-awareness-and-system-justification

7. Matthew 26:11

8. Proverbs 18:23

9. https://blogs.worldbank.org/opendata/half-world-s-poor-live-just-5-countries

10. https://theculturetrip.com/africa/south-africa/articles/what-to-know-about-the-khoisan-south-africas-first-people/

11. Herbert, Trevor, The Church, The City & The Virus, Chapter 17

12. https://www.gfmag.com/global-data/economic-data/richest-countries-in-the-world

13. https://www.investopedia.com/insights/worlds-top-economies/

14. https://www.usatoday.com/story/money/2018/11/29/poorest-countries-world-2018/38429473/

15. https://www.theguardian.com/technology/2017/feb/18/bill-gates-warns-tens-of-millions-could-be-killed-by-bio-terrorism

16. https://www.businessinsider.com/fauci-warned-trump-infectious-disease-pandemic-danger-2017-2020-4?IR=T

17. https://www.gatesfoundation.org/goalkeepers/report/2020-report/#GlobalPerspective

18. https://www.gapminder.org/answers/how-many-are-rich-and-how-many-are-poor/

19. https://www.dailymaverick.co.za/article/2020-06-10-who-is-in-charge-the-nccc-or-the-cabinet-ramaphosa-unveils-the-blurring-of-democratic-practice-at-the-highest-level/

20. https://www.dailymaverick.co.za/article/2020-02-12-south-africas-state-of-unemployment-disaster/

21. https://www.iol.co.za/business-report/economy/3-million-people-became-unemployed-between-february-and-april-51000019

22. Business Day 4 September 2020

23. https://ourworldindata.org/causes-of-death#what-do-people-die-from

24. Herbert, Trevor, The Church, The City & The Virus

25. https://citychanger.org/

26. Matthew 28:19-20

27. Courageous Leadership, Bill Hybels

28. Isaiah 40:31

29. Sachs, Jeffrey, The end of poverty, How we can make it happen in our lifetime

30. https://www.weforum.org/events/world-economic-forum-annual-meeting-2020

31. https://www.cidrap.umn.edu/news-perspective/2020/02/philippines-has-first-ncov-death-outside-china-cases-top-14000

32. https://www.bbc.com/news/world-asia-china-51482994

33. https://www.businessinsider.com/fauci-warned-trump-infectious-disease-pandemic-danger-2017-2020-4?IR=T

34. Orwell, George, Animal Farm, 1945

35. https://www.in-mind.org/article/fair-enough-the-inequality-paradox-inequality-awareness-and-system-justification

36. https://gigaconnect.org/

37. https://www.gov.za/issues/national-development-plan-2030

38. https://businesstech.co.za/news/government/434851/south-africa-does-not-have-a-viable-economic-recovery-plan-analyst/

39. https://www.un.org/sustainabledevelopment/sustainable-development-goals/

40. https://www.gov.za/sites/default/files/Executive%20Summary-NDP%202030%20-%20Our%20future%20-%20make%20it%20work.pdf

41. Margaret Mead was an American cultural anthropologist who featured frequently as an author and speaker in the mass media during the 1960s and 1970s. Born: 16 December 1901, Philadelphia, Pennsylvania, United StatesDied: 15 November 1978, Hospital, New York, United States

42. 2 Corinthians 4:7

43. Herbert, Trevor The Church, The City & The Virus, Chapter 33

44. Shakespeare William, Julius Caesar Act IV, scene ii

45. Bruce Theron, The Church, The City & The Virus

46. Nehemiah 2:10

47. https://www.desiderata.com/desiderata.html

48. Jeremiah 20:9

49. Luke 19:44

50. Esther 4:14

51. Matthew 9: 36

52. Acts 4:32

53. Acts 5:29

54. https://www.biola.edu/blogs/good-book-blog/2020/how-did-early-christians-respond-to-plagues

55. Genesis 1:28

56. Herbert, Trevor, The Church, The City & The Virus, Chapter 33

57. Matthew 11:18-19
58. Matthew 8:19-20
59. Matthew 18:11
60. Matthew 9:36
61. Luke 13:32
62. John 19:11
63. John 10:18

# By the Same Author

*Three New Publications*
**Coming Soon!**

**December 2020, March 2021 and June 2021 (DV)**

December 2020
**Transformation in the South African Workplace - Has the Project Failed?**
After the author's recent publication, there were so many enquiries about his first work, *Affirmative Action in the South African Workplace*, this new revised and updated version will be released for some holiday reading before Christmas - a great gift for those friends who are passionate about the true transformation of South Africa.

March 2021
**Life Begins at 60 - And Other Truths**
The author takes the reader on a biographical journey that spans more than sixty years and also reveals the personal life-changing moments during the year 2020 that made him turn to writing again after more than a quarter century. Besides some very personal revelations, there are also many leadership lessons from which those currently in leadership positions stand to benefit.

June 2021
**The Church at Large - Free, Un-captured**
In his recent work *The Church, The City & The Virus - Where was the Church?* the author provided his readers with his unique definition of the phrase, 'Church at Large'. In this powerful and almost prophetic work, he further unpacks this definition and paints a picture of a future where the Church has regained her prophetic voice again.

## About the Author

Trevor Herbert is a former senior executive in the retail sector who opted for full-time pastoral ministry in the year 2000. Currently he serves as a pastor in the Apostolic Faith Mission of South Africa (AFM of SA), one of the larger denominations in South Africa (1.4 million members). The AFM of SA has a footprint in Africa, Asia and Australia, as well as parts of Europe and the USA.

Trevor is also involved in several city and community-impacting organisations, as well as local and global ecumenical initiatives. He lives in Cape Town, South Africa, and is a father of three children, two sons-in-law and grandfather of two grandsons. He is married to Moira (a retired nurse) for 37 years. The family resides in the northern suburbs of Cape Town. This is his third book after his first work, *Affirmative Action in the South Africa Workplace* was published in 1994 and his recent work *The Church, The City & The Virus - Where was the Church?* during July 2020.

First print October 2020

www.ingramcontent.com/pod-product-compliance
Lightning Source LLC
Chambersburg PA
CBHW071309060426
42444CB00034B/1740